a bag of marbles

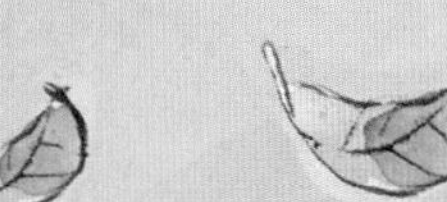

Based on the memoir by **JOSEPH JOFFO**

Adapted by **KRIS**

Illustrated by **VINCENT BAILLY**

Translated by **EDWARD GAUVIN**

GRAPHIC UNIVERSE™ • MINNEAPOLIS

For us. All of us.

Dedicated to all those who know why they fought,

and those still fighting today.

—K. and V.B.

Happy as God in France.

—Yiddish proverb

First American edition published in 2013 by Graphic Universe™.
Published by arrangement with Futuropolis.

Graphic Universe™
A division of Lerner Publishing Group, Inc.
241 First Avenue North
Minneapolis, MN 55401 U.S.A.

Website address: www.lernerbooks.com

Main body text set in Andy
Typeface provided by Monotype Typography

Library of Congress Cataloging-in-Publication Data

Kris, 1972–
[Sac de billes. English]
A bag of marbles : the graphic novel / based on the novel by Joseph Joffo ; adapted by Kris ; illustrated by Vincent Bailly ; translated by Edward Gauvin.
p. cm
Summary: In 1941, ten-year-old Joseph Joffo and his older brother, Maurice, must hide their Jewish heritage and undertake a long and dangerous journey from Nazi-occupied Paris to reach their other brothers in the free zone.
ISBN 978–1–4677–0700–8 (lib. bdg. : alk. paper)
ISBN 978–1–4677–1651–2 (eBook)
1. Joffo, Joseph—Juvenile fiction. 2. Joffo, Maurice—Juvenile fiction. 3. Holocaust, Jewish (1939–1945)—France—Juvenile fiction. 4. Graphic novels. [1. Graphic novels. 2. Joffo, Joseph—Fiction. 3. Joffo, Maurice—Fiction. 4. Holocaust, Jewish (1939–1945)—France—Fiction. 5. Jews—France—Fiction. 6. World War, 1939–1945—France—Fiction. 7. France—History—German occupation, 1940–1945—Fiction.] I. Bailly, Vincent, illustrator. II. Gauvin, Edward. III. Joffo, Joseph. Sac de billes. IV. Title.
PZ7.7.K74Bag 2013
741.5'944—dc23 [B] 2013002284

Manufactured in the United States of America
1 – DP – 7/15/13

ÊTES-VOUS
PLUS FRANÇAIS
POPULATIONS
abandonnées,
faites confiance
AU SOLDAT ALLEMAND

part one

C'MON, JO, WILL YOU GO ALREADY?
WHAT THE HECK'S TAKING YOU SO LONG?
BOULANGERIE
PATISSERIE
CAFÉ BAR
HTEL
REVOLUTIO
NATIONAL

GO AHEAD, CRACK WISE. I JUST LOST SEVEN MARBLES, AND THIS IS MY LAST ONE! IT'S MY LUCKY ONE TOO . . .
SO WHAT? I'M NOT GOING TO SIT HERE ON MY KEISTER ALL DAY.
POC
PARIS, RUE MARCADET, 1941 . . .
GRAND HOTEL DU NORD
CAFE
TABAC
AW, QUIT YOUR BLUBBERING.

I'M NOT.
WHEN YOU LOOK AWAY LIKE THAT I CAN ALWAYS TELL YOU'RE BLUBBERING.
HERE, TAKE IT.
TEN-YEAR-OLDS DON'T CRY OVER MARBLES.
WE BETTER HURRY. WE WERE SUPPOSED TO BE HOME HALF AN HOUR AGO! WE'RE GONNA GET IT!
DING
JO, MAURICE! MY LITTLE HOOLIGANS, HOME AT LAST.
HOMEWORK! HOP TO IT! YOUR MOTHER'S GOING TO HAVE A FIT.

YOU DONE YET?
HOLD YOUR HORSES! WE'VE BEEN AT IT LESS THAN A MINUTE. IF WE DON'T DRAG IT OUT A LITTLE, MAMA WILL JUST SEND US BACK HERE.
OK, THAT SHOULD BE LONG ENOUGH. LET'S GO!
DONE ALREADY?
EASIER THAN A BUZZ CUT, RIGHT, ALBERT?
WHERE TO?
DO SOME DOORBELL DITCHES? HEAD DOWN TO THE CANAL?

* WHY NOT HERE?
** SURE LOOKS GOOD TO ME. LET'S GO!

* JEWISH BUSINESS

IF WHOEVER'S NEXT WOULD PLEASE HAVE A SEAT...
THANKS.
WOULD YOU LIKE IT SHORT?
YES. AND PARTED TO THE RIGHT, PLEASE.

* THE MAN KNOWS KARLSRUHE! HE IS FROM ALSACE!

ARE THOSE YOUR BOYS?
YES. THEY'RE LITTLE HOODLUMS.
THE WAR IS ROTTEN. THE JEWS ARE TO BLAME.
YOU THINK SO?
I'M SURE OF IT.
VOILÀ!
THERE YOU ARE. ALL DONE.
VERY GOOD. THANKS!
YOU'RE HAPPY WITH YOUR HAIRCUTS?
VERY GOOD. EXCELLENT.
BEFORE YOU GO, I SHOULD TELL YOU THIS. ALL THESE PEOPLE HERE ARE JEWS.

I WAS TALKING
ABOUT RICH
JEWS.
Jüdisches
Geschäft

NOW, WHERE WERE WE?
THE ADVENTURES OF YOUR GRANDFATHER, JACOB JOFFO.
WHERE DID I LEAVE OFF?
THE POGROMS WERE STARTING!
AH, YES.
THE POGROMS WERE STARTING.
ALL THIS HAPPENED LONG AGO, IN THE RUSSIAN PART OF BESSARABIA . . .
OF ALL OUR CHILDHOOD MEMORIES—MAURICE'S AND MINE—THESE FAMILY STORY NIGHTS WERE AMONG THE BEST.
10

MY GRANDFATHER'S ADVENTURES, INTERLOCKED LIKE NESTING DOLLS, WERE SET AGAINST A BACKDROP OF DESERTS WHITE WITH SNOW AND TWISTING ALLEYWAYS IN TOWNS STREWN WITH GILDED CUPOLAS.

HE HAD TWELVE SONS. HE WAS RICH, GENEROUS, HAPPY, AND RESPECTED IN HIS VILLAGE SOUTH OF ODESSA . . . UNTIL THE DAY THE POGROMS BEGAN.

I ENVISIONED BRANDISHED RIFLE BUTTS AND FLEEING PEASANTS. BEFORE MY EYES PLAYED WHIRLWINDS OF FLAME AND SABER BLADES, AND TOWERING OVER IT ALL WAS THE COLOSSAL FIGURE OF MY GRANDFATHER.

AT NIGHT, DISGUISED AS A PEASANT AND WITH THE CLEAR CONSCIENCE OF A RIGHTEOUS MAN WHO WON'T STAND BY WHILE HIS FRIENDS ARE KILLED, HE WOULD BEAT UP SOLDIERS. THEN HE'D HEAD HOME, WHISTLING A YIDDISH TUNE.

BUT THEN THE MASSACRES GOT WORSE. MY GRANDFATHER UNDERSTOOD THAT ALL BY HIMSELF HE COULD NOT KNOCK OUT THE THREE BATTALIONS THAT THE CZAR HAD SENT TO THE AREA. THE WHOLE FAMILY HAD TO FLEE—AND FAST.

WHAT FOLLOWED WAS A LIVELY AND PICTURESQUE PROGRESSION ACROSS ALL OF EUROPE, FULL OF STORMY NIGHTS, REVELRY, LAUGHTER, TEARS, AND DEATH.

AND THEN ONE DAY, THEY CROSSED THE LAST BORDER. THERE WERE FIELDS OF WHEAT, SINGING BIRDS, AND BRIGHT VILLAGES WITH RED ROOFTOPS AND A STEEPLE.

ON THE BIGGEST HOUSE WAS AN INSCRIPTION: ***LIBERTÉ, ÉGALITÉ, FRATERNITÉ.*** THEN FEAR LEFT THE REFUGEES, FOR THEY KNEW THEY HAD ARRIVED.

THAT NIGHT WE LISTENED AS WE USUALLY DID: RIVETED, MOUTHS WIDE OPEN.
THE LOVE THE FRENCH PEOPLE HAVE FOR THEIR COUNTRY COMES SO NATURALLY. BUT I KNOW OF NO ONE WHO EVER LOVED THAT COUNTRY AS MUCH AS MY PARENTS, WHO WERE BORN FIVE THOUSAND MILES AWAY.
AH . . . IF YOUR MOTHER'S HERE, IT MUST MEAN IT'S PAST YOUR BEDTIME. OFF TO SLEEP!
NOT YET. I WAS JUST WONDERING . . .
YOU . . . YOU DON'T THINK THERE'LL BE TROUBLE NOW THAT THE GERMANS ARE HERE?
NO, NOT HERE. NOT IN FRANCE. NEVER.
SO LONG AS THE WORDS **LIBERTÉ, ÉGALITÉ, FRATERNITÉ** ARE WRITTEN ON OUR TOWN HALLS, WE'LL BE ALL RIGHT HERE.
GOOD NIGHT, CHILDREN.
GOOD NIGHT . . .
Sanitätspark 541
Der Militärbefehlshaber in Frankreich
LIBERTE
RF
EGALITE
RF
FRATERNITE

YOUR TURN, JO.
Juif*
C'MON, YOU DON'T WANT TO BE LATE FOR SCHOOL!
DON'T CRY. YOU'LL GET YOUR GOLD MEDAL TOO!
THE MOVIES, THE TRAIN . . . WHY DON'T THEY BAN US FROM PLAYING MARBLES TOO?
HMPH! I WISH THEY'D BAN US FROM GOING TO SCHOOL!
THAT'S ENOUGH, MAURICE.
VOILÀ, JO. YOU'RE ALL SET.
DO YOU KNOW WHAT YOU HAVE TO DO NOW?
BE FIRST IN OUR CLASS.
TO PISS HITLER OFF!
SURE. YOU COULD PUT IT THAT WAY.

* JEW

EXPOSITION
LE JUIF ET LA FRANCE
WILL WE HAVE TO WEAR THESE LONG?
BEATS ME.
WHY? DOES IT BOTHER YOU?
WHY WOULD IT? IT DOESN'T WEIGH MUCH. IT DOESN'T SLOW ME DOWN, SO—
JUIF
SO IF IT DOESN'T BOTHER YOU, HOW COME YOU'VE GOT YOUR SCARF OVER IT?
I ALWAYS WEAR MY SCARF IN FRONT. THE WIND JUST BLEW IT THAT WAY.
YEAH, SURE, BUDDY. THE WIND.
HEY, JOFFO!
SALUT, ZERATI.
SALUT—
HOLY MOLY!
JUIF
JESUS, YOU'RE LUCKY! THAT STAR SURE IS A BEAUT!

HEY, FELLAS! GET A LOAD OF JOFFO!

YOU'RE NOT THE ONLY ONE. SOME OLDER KIDS GOT THEM TOO.

HEY, YOU A KIKE?

IT'S ON ACCOUNT OF THE KIKES THERE'S A WAR ON.

YOU'RE A REAL MORON! YOU THINK THIS WAR'S ALL JO'S FAULT?

SURE DO! WE GOTTA GET RID OF ALL THE YIDS!
YOU SEE THE NOSE ON HIM?
WHAT'S WRONG WITH MY NOSE? IT'S THE SAME AS IT WAS YESTERDAY!
IN LINE, CHILDREN! SINGLE FILE!

CLOSE YOUR NOTEBOOKS NOW. AGAIN, FROM MEMORY: THE RHÔNE VALLEY...
THE RHÔNE VALLEY DIVIDES THE ANCIENT MOUNTAIN MASSES OF THE MASSIF CENTRAL FROM—
DI DILING
C'MON, JO, HURRY UP! RECESS!
HEY, KIKE!
HEY, KIKE! KIKE!
KIKE! KIKE!
KIKE!
ALL RIGHT, WHAT'S GOING ON HERE? BEAT IT, YOU TWO! SCRAM!
...INDEED, ONE MIGHT SAY THIS IS WHERE THE FUTURE OF FRANCE LIES.
WORK, FAMILY, COUNTRY...
UN PETIT FRANÇAIS REGARDE BIEN EN FACE

JO!
I'LL TRADE YOU.
TRADE ME WHAT?
FOR YOUR STAR!
SURE.
HERE.
ALL RIGHT! THANKS!

NO SCHOOL THIS AFTERNOON.
REALLY? BUT WE LEFT OUR SCHOOLBAGS—
DON'T WORRY. I'LL GO GET THEM. YOU'RE FREE FOR THE REST OF THE DAY.
BUT BE HOME BEFORE DARK.
I HAVE SOMETHING TO TELL YOU.

C'MON, IT'S GETTING LATE.
HEY! PAPA CLOSED UP SHOP ALREADY!
PAPA?
COME ON UP! I'M IN YOUR ROOM.
UH . . . WE'RE HOME, PAPA.
YES. SIT DOWN. LET ME TELL YOU A STORY.
FOR ONCE, I'M GOING TO TELL YOU MY STORY.
AS A BOY, I LIVED IN RUSSIA. THE CZAR RULED OVER RUSSIA. HE LIKED MAKING WAR, AND TO DO SO, HE SENT OUT EMISSARIES TO ROUND UP LITTLE BOYS AND MAKE SOLDIERS OF THEM.
NOW, I DIDN'T WANT TO BE A SOLDIER. I KNEW I'D BE MISTREATED. SO WHEN I WAS OLD ENOUGH TO GO, MY FATHER TOOK ME ASIDE . . .
. . . AS I'M DOING WITH YOU, TONIGHT.
19

YOUR MOTHER'S STORY IS A BIT LIKE MINE. IT'S QUITE ORDINARY, IN FACT. I MET HER IN PARIS. WE FELL IN LOVE, GOT MARRIED, AND HAD YOU.

YES, MY SONS. YOU'RE GOING TO GO AWAY. TODAY IT'S YOUR TURN.

AND THE GERMANS ARE WORSE THAN THE RUSSIANS. TODAY, A YELLOW STAR, TOMORROW COME THE ARRESTS. WE HAVE TO RUN.

WHAT ABOUT YOU AND MAMA?
DON'T WORRY. THE RUSSIANS DIDN'T GET ME AT SEVEN. THE NAZIS WON'T GET ME AT FIFTY.
YOUR BROTHERS HAVE ALREADY MADE IT TO THE FREE ZONE. YOU'LL LEAVE TONIGHT. MAMA AND I STILL HAVE A FEW THINGS TO TAKE CARE OF, AND THEN WE'LL GO TOO.
NOW, REMEMBER WHAT I'M TELLING YOU: TONIGHT, TAKE THE METRO TO THE GARE D'AUSTERLITZ. THERE, YOU'LL BUY A TICKET TO DAX.
RIGHT BY DAX IS A VILLAGE CALLED HAGETMAU. LOOK FOR A PASSEUR THERE. THEY'LL TAKE PEOPLE LIKE YOU, PEOPLE WITHOUT PAPERS, OVER THE LINE.
ONCE YOU'RE ON THE OTHER SIDE, YOU'RE IN UNOCCUPIED FRANCE. YOU'LL BE SAFE.
YOUR BROTHERS ARE IN MENTON, BY THE ITALIAN BORDER. YOU'LL FIND THEM THERE. WE'RE GIVING YOU EACH 5,000 FRANCS.
LE TOUR DE LA FRANCE PAR DEUX ENFANTS
COURS MOYEN
PAR
G. BRUNO
PARIS
5,000 FRANCS!
YOU'LL NEED EVERY CENT.
THERE'S ONE MORE THING YOU HAVE TO KNOW. YOU'RE JEWS, BUT YOU MUST NEVER **EVER** ADMIT IT. YOU HEAR? **NEVER!**
COME HERE, JOSEPH.
ARE YOU A JEW?
NO.

DON'T LIE! ARE YOU A JEW, JOSEPH?
NO!
ALL RIGHT THEN. I THINK I'VE TOLD YOU EVERYTHING.
PAPA?
YES, JOSEPH?
WHAT IS . . . A JEW?
WELL, IT'S KIND OF EMBARRASSING, BUT . . . I DON'T REALLY KNOW.
ALL RIGHT, THEN . . .
LONG AGO, WE LIVED IN ONE COUNTRY. WE WERE DRIVEN FROM IT AND SORT OF SCATTERED ALL OVER THE WORLD.
EVERY SO OFTEN, WE ARE DRIVEN OUT AGAIN. AND SO WE HAVE TO GO AWAY AND HIDE.
UNTIL THEY GET TIRED OF HUNTING US DOWN.

DONG
DONG
WELL, YOU'RE ALL SET. IN YOUR KNAPSACK YOU'LL FIND MONEY AND AN ADDRESS FOR HENRI AND ALBERT.
SAY GOOD-BYE TO YOUR MOTHER AND GO.
AU REVOIR, MAURICE.
AU REVOIR, JO. SEE YOU SOON.
AW, C'MON! YOU'D THINK THEY WERE NEWBORNS LEAVING THE NEST FOR GOOD! GO ON NOW. SEE YOU SOON, BOYS!
23

OVER HERE! HURRY!
IT'S LONGER THIS WAY BUT LESS CROWDED.
AND NOW, TIME TO SPOT THE NICEST GUY CLOSE TO THE FRONT.
MONSIEUR, MY LITTLE BROTHER . . . HE'S GOT A BAD FOOT. WE COME FROM FAR AWAY . . . COULD YOU . . .?
GO AHEAD, KIDS. MY TRAIN WON'T ARRIVE FOR A WHILE.
TWO FOR DAX ONE-WAY, THIRD CLASS.
Saint Jean 20"08
via Dax 21"10
TRACK 7. WE'VE STILL GOT HALF AN HOUR. LET'S TRY AND FIND SEATS.

* RESERVED FOR GERMAN SOLDIERS

GOING FAR, CHILDREN?
TO DAX.

WHAT ARE YOUR NAMES?
JOSEPH MARTIN. AND HE'S MAURICE MARTIN.

SKREEEE
DAX! LAST STOP!
LOTS OF PEOPLE JUMPED OFF WHEN THE TRAIN SLOWED DOWN.
C'MON. LET'S WAIT INSIDE THE COMPARTMENT.
27

HALT!
HALT!
PAPERS.
PAPERS.

FATHER, WE DON'T HAVE ANY PAPERS.

IF YOU LOOK SCARED, THE GERMANS WILL NOTICE THAT WITHOUT YOUR TELLING THEM. COME HERE, CHILDREN.

PAPERS.

PAPERS.

PAPERS.

DANKE. *

THIS IS ALL YOU HAVE?
OUI, MONSIEUR.

TAKE YOUR SUITCASE AND GO OUT IN THE HALLWAY.

DANKE.

* THANK YOU.

IS THAT REALLY YOU?
YES. I'VE LOST SOME WEIGHT, BUT THAT'S ME.
AH, THE WAR, THE RATIONING . . . BUT PRIESTS DON'T EAT MUCH.
THAT'S NOT TRUE AT ALL, AT LEAST IN MY CASE.
OH, THE CHILDREN ARE WITH ME.
HA HA! FINE. BUT DON'T LET YOURSELF GO, FATHER. PEOPLE NEED YOU!
WE CAN GET OFF NOW. WHERE ARE YOU HEADED?
HAGETMAU. FROM THERE WE'LL TRY TO CROSS THE LINE.
GOOD. LET'S HAVE SOME BREAKFAST AT THE STATION, AND THEN I'LL TAKE YOU TO THE BUS.
30

WHAT DID I DO?

YOU LIED TO SAVE US. YOU SAID WE WERE WITH YOU.

GO ON NOW. HURRY. SOMETIMES IN LIFE YOU NEED TO.

HAGETMAU
CRIPES, IT SURE IS DEAD AROUND HERE!
DONG
DONG
DONG
OH, RIGHT. NOON! EVERYBODY'S EATING LUNCH.
UH . . .
WE COULD STOP FOR A BITE TOO, RIGHT?
YOU'RE RIGHT, LET'S GO. DON'T WANT TO DIE OF HUNGER.
32

SHUT THE DOOR, KIDS! WE'RE NOT TRYING TO HEAT THE SIDEWALK! WHAT DO YOU WANT?
WE WANT LUNCH!
THEN RIGHT THIS WAY! THERE'S A TABLE IN THE BACK!
WE'VE GOT LENTILS WITH BACON AND STUFFED EGGPLANT. CHEESE OR FRUIT FOR DESSERT AND RADISHES WITH SALT FOR STARTERS. THAT OK?
GREAT, THANKS!
WE'RE GOING TO RUN INTO EVERYONE FROM RUE MARCADET HERE. THEY'RE ALL PEOPLE LIKE US: JEWS ON THE RUN.
EAT YOUR DESSERT. LET'S NOT HANG AROUND.
33

GOOD THING WE'RE NOT STAYING IN THIS TOWN. WITH WHAT THEY SERVE, WE'D TURN INTO SKELETONS! MY RADISHES WERE HOLLOW, AND I'M STILL LOOKING FOR THE BACON IN THOSE LENTILS.

DON'T WORRY, WE'LL TRY CROSSING TONIGHT. IT SHOULD BE LESS DANGEROUS IN THE DARK.
BUT FIRST WE HAVE TO FIND A PASSEUR.
BONJOUR, MADAME HUDOT! HERE'S YOUR ORDER!
MERCI, MADAME HUDOT! AU REVOIR, MADAME HUDOT! SEE YOU NEXT TIME!
WELL, LOOKY HERE.

HEY! HOW 'BOUT SOME INFORMATION?
?!

I'LL TELL YOU BEFORE YOU EVEN ASK. LOOKING FOR A PASSEUR?
UH . . . YEAH.

PIECE OF CAKE! LEAVE TOWN ON THE MAIN ROAD, AND FIRST FARM ON YOUR RIGHT, ASK FOR OLD BEDARD. 5,000 FRANCS A PERSON.

5,000 FRANCS!

THERE'S ANOTHER WAY. RAYMOND WILL TAKE YOU FOR JUST 500 SMACKERS. RAYMOND, THAT'S ME.
BUT YOU HAVE TO FINISH MY MEAT DELIVERIES FOR ME. THE ADDRESSES ARE ON THE PACKAGES, AND YOU HAVE TO COLLECT TIPS. HOW'S THAT SOUND?

IT SOUNDED GOOD.
MEET UP AT TEN TONIGHT!
UNDER THE BRIDGE BY THE ARCH! CAN'T MISS IT. THERE'S ONLY ONE!
DO WE HAVE ENOUGH MONEY?
SURE, WE HAVE IT! BUT WE'LL BE BROKE AFTER THAT.
EH, DOESN'T MATTER. ONCE WE'RE IN THE FREE ZONE, WE'LL MANAGE. JUST THINK! IF WE HADN'T MET THAT GUY, AT 5,000 A HEAD, WE'D BE STUCK!
MEANWHILE, WE'VE GOT MEAT TO DELIVER!

PSST!

DON'T BE FRIGHTENED. I . . . I WON'T HURT YOU.

YOU FROM AROUND HERE?
NO.
ARE YOU JEWISH?
NO.

I AM. MY WIFE AND HER MOTHER ARE IN THE WOODS. I'M TRYING TO GET ACROSS.
WHAT HAPPENED TO YOU?

A PASSEUR DITCHED US IN THE WOODS IN THE MIDDLE OF THE NIGHT ABOUT TWENTY MILES FROM HERE. I FELL DOWN TRYING TO GRAB HIM. HE TOOK 20,000 FRANCS. WE'VE BEEN WALKING EVER SINCE.

LOOK, WE'RE TRYING TO CROSS TOO. MEET US AT TEN UNDER THE BRIDGE AT THE OTHER END OF TOWN. YOU CAN ASK OUR GUIDE IF HE'LL TAKE YOU TOO.

THANK YOU! THANK YOU WITH ALL MY HEART! WE'RE SO TIRED . . .

I HOPE IT WORKS. SEE YOU TONIGHT! THANK YOU, THANK YOU!
36

WE'D BETTER BE CAREFUL. SOME PEOPLE AROUND HERE HAVE A FUNNY WAY OF EARNING A LIVING.
YOU THINK RAYMOND WOULD . . .
I DON'T KNOW, BUT I'M GONNA WATCH OUT.
WE'VE GOT TO STAY RIGHT ON TOP OF HIM.
CRACK
OH, THERE YOU ARE. RAYMOND SHOULDN'T BE LONG.
YEAH, UNLESS HE . . .
SHH! LISTEN!
IT'S HIM! NOT EXACTLY LOW PROFILE . . .
HELLO! HEY, DID YOU MULTIPLY DURING THE DAY?
THESE PEOPLE WANT TO CROSS TOO. THEY'RE EXHAUSTED AND THEY HAVE MONEY.
FINE BY ME. THREE OF YOU? THIS IS A GOOD NIGHT! USUALLY THE OTHER PASSEURS DON'T LEAVE ME THIS MANY!
C'MON, LET'S GO!

CRACK
OOPS!
DON'T WORRY, LI'L BUDDY! NO NEED TO BE JUMPY. JUST FOLLOW ME, DO WHAT I DO, AND DON'T WORRY ABOUT THE REST!
UH . . . RAYMOND? I THINK THERE'S SOMEONE ON OUR RIGHT.
YEAH, A DOZEN SOMEONES. WE'LL LET THEM GET AHEAD OF US AND THEN FOLLOW. WE CAN SIT DOWN FOR A MOMENT.
IS IT STILL FAR?
IF WE WENT STRAIGHT, WE'D BE THERE IN A JIFFY. BUT WE HAVE TO CIRCLE THE CLEARING.
38

OK, WE'RE CLEAR. LET'S GO!
NOW, FOLLOW THIS TRAIL. IN MAYBE TWO HUNDRED YARDS, YOU'LL REACH A DITCH. WATCH OUT, IT'S DEEP AND FULL OF WATER. PAST THAT, YOU'LL FIND A FARMHOUSE.
PERFECT! THIS WAY, EVERYONE!
GO ON IN, EVEN IF IT'S DARK. THE FARMER KNOWS WHAT'S GOING ON. YOU CAN SLEEP IN THE HAY, AND YOU WON'T BE COLD.
YOU MEAN . . . THAT'S THE FREE ZONE OVER THERE?
THE FREE ZONE?
HA, YOU'RE IN IT ALREADY!

BUT. . . IS IT USUALLY THIS EASY? I THOUGHT THERE'D BE WATCHTOWERS, BARBED WIRE, PATROLS WITH DOGS . . .

YOU ALMOST SOUND DISAPPOINTED! NO, IT'S NOTHING LIKE THAT. USUALLY IT GOES REAL SMOOTH. THE GUARD POSTS ARE FAR APART, AND THE ONLY DANGER'S FROM PATROLS.

BUT THEY HAVE TO GO BY THE FORD NEAR THE BADIN FARM, AND WHEN HE SEES THEM, THE OLD MAN SENDS HIS SON TO WARN US.

NOW DON'T GO THINKING IT'S THIS EASY ALL OVER. LESS THAN FIFTEEN MILES FROM HERE, SOME PEOPLE WERE KILLED RECENTLY. IT'S GETTING HARDER ALL THE TIME.

AU REVOIR! AND SAFE TRAVELS!

THIS IS THE PLACE, BOYS.
?!
THERE'S STRAW IN THE SHED AND BLANKETS BEHIND THE DOOR.
SLEEP AS LONG AS YOU WANT.
YOU NEED ANYTHING, JUST KNOCK ON THE LITTLE WINDOW BEHIND THE HENHOUSE. SEE IT? THAT'S WHERE I SLEEP. GO ON. GOOD NIGHT.
GOT IT. THANKS! GOOD NIGHT, MONSIEUR!

* I'LL BE BACK. DON'T SAY ANYTHING TO ANYONE.

I WENT BACK ACROSS AND BROUGHT MORE REFUGEES OVER.
YOU WHAT?!
I WENT BACK AND FORTH EIGHT TIMES. I GOT A HANDLE ON THE ROUTE.
I BROUGHT OVER A GOOD FORTY PEOPLE. BUT IT'S LIGHT OUT NOW. I NEED TO SLEEP.
ARE YOU CRAZY? WHAT IF YOU WERE CAUGHT? WHY'D YOU DO IT?
JUST BECAUSE WE'RE IN THE FREE ZONE DOESN'T MEAN WE WON'T NEED MONEY FOR FOOD AND TRAVEL.
HERE, 20,000 SMACKERS! GO AHEAD, COUNT!
AND NOW, LET ME SLEEP. I ASKED AROUND: WE TAKE THE TRAIN TO MARSEILLE FROM AIRE-SUR-L'ADOUR, AND THAT'S NOT EXACTLY NEXT DOOR.
SIXTEEN MILES ON FOOT, IT WEARS OUT, IT WEARS OUT...
43

. . . IT WEARS OUT YOUR SHOES.
SEVENTEEN MILES ON FOOT . . .
SEVENTEEN MILES! ARE YOU KIDDING? WE HAVEN'T EVEN GONE THREE!
WANT SOME BREAD?
NOT WHILE WE'RE WALKING. ANY ATHLETE KNOWS THAT. IT BREAKS YOUR STRIDE!
BUT WE'RE NOT ATHLETES!
NO, BUT WE STILL HAVE A WAYS TO GO. BETTER NOT.
D2
AIRE SUR L'ADOUR 18
D2
YOU LIMPING?
DON'T WORRY.
EIGHTEEN MILES ON FOOT . . .
D2
AIRE SUR L'ADOUR 17
44

OK, ENOUGH, STOP!
?
D2
D2
I'M TOTALLY BEAT. DIDN'T GET ENOUGH SLEEP.
OK. REST A LITTLE. YOU'LL FEEL BETTER LATER. THERE'S NO RUSH.
YOU LOOK LIKE A GOOD OL' PARISIAN MUTT! DON'T KNOW WHERE YOU'RE FROM, BUT YOU COULD BE JEWISH TOO!
AW, CRUD . . . JUST WHAT I THOUGHT! DARN BLISTER!
THIS MIGHT HELP.
NNGH.
AHH, THAT'S BETTER—
CREEE
CREEEAK

WHOA!
PARDON ME, MONSIEUR. WOULD YOU BE GOING TO AIRE-SUR-L'ADOUR BY ANY CHANCE?
AS A MATTER OF FACT, I AM. TO BE PRECISE, I'M GOING WITHIN A MILE OF THERE.
UM . . .
WOULD YOU . . . I MEAN, COULD ME AND MY BROTHER RIDE IN YOUR BUGGY?
MY DEAR FELLOW, THIS IS NO BUGGY. IT'S A BAROUCHE!
OH . . . SORRY.
KNOW THIS: YOU'RE NEVER TOO YOUNG TO LEARN TO CALL THINGS BY THEIR PROPER NAMES. BUT IT DOESN'T MATTER. YOU MAY RIDE WITH ME.
?!
THANKS, MONSIEUR!
CRIMINY! WHERE'D YOU FIND THIS GUY?

AS YOU CAN SEE, OUR SPEED IS LIMITED AND THE COMFORT RUDIMENTARY. BUT IT'S STILL BETTER THAN WALKING. MY CAR WAS REQUISITIONED FOR SOME OFFICER IN THE OCCUPIED ZONE.

YOU SEE, CHILDREN, WHEN A COUNTRY LOSES A WAR SO CLEARLY AND DECISIVELY, IT'S BECAUSE THE LEADERS FAILED TO MEASURE UP.

LET ME MAKE IT PLAIN: THE REPUBLIC FAILED TO MEASURE UP!

WHAT FRANCE LACKED WAS A GREAT REACTIONARY NATIONAL MOVEMENT, WHICH WOULD HAVE ENABLED HER TO RECOVER HER STRENGTH AND FAITH. THAT'S WHAT WE NEEDED TO DRIVE THE HUN BACK ACROSS THE BORDER!

YOUNG MEN, YOU HAVE LISTENED TO ME POLITELY AND ATTENTIVELY.

D2
AIRE SUR L'ADOUR 2 Km

SPLENDIDE
HOTEL
DAMN . . .
MARSEILLE, HERE WE COME!
PATHÉ PALACE
3 SALLES
LAINE
PATHÉ
HEY, MAURICE! LOOK!
PATH
TICKETS ARE PRETTY CHEAP . . .
48

Le film en couleurs le plus prodigieux du siècle
aventures fantastiques DU BARON Munchhausen
HANS ALBERS
WE HAVE SOME TIME TO KILL. THE TRAIN FOR MENTON'S NOT TILL TONIGHT. BUT THE FIRST SHOW'S NOT TILL TEN.
SO LET'S HIT THE STREETS AND COME BACK LATER!
LE FRANÇAIS
TABACS
CIGARES
CAFÉ DE LA
GLACI
SHIT.
WHOA!
THE SEA...
V ET SPIRITUEUX

HEY, KIDS, EVER BEEN TO THE CHÂTEAU D'IF?
HOP ON BOARD AND I'LL TAKE YOU THERE! HALF PRICE!
IN THAT LITTLE THING? WE'D GET SEASICK.
HA HA! YOU'RE PROBABLY RIGHT. THE WAY YOU TALK, YOU'RE PROBABLY NOT FROM AROUND HERE, ARE YOU?
NO, WE'RE FROM PARIS.
WELL, AT LEAST TAKE THE FERRY ACROSS THE HARBOR! IT'LL GIVE YOU A TASTE OF THINGS!

BAR
HEY!

HEE HEE! NICE BERET YOU'VE GOT THERE, CUTIE!
WHOOPS! YOUR TURN, MARIA!
COME UP AND GET IT, HONEY!
WELL, WHAT ARE YOU WAITING FOR? IN A FEW YEARS I'LL TAKE OFF THE REST, YOU KNOW! **HA HA!**
la lune
MARIA, THEY'RE KIDS! YOU SHOULD BE ASHAMED OF YOURSELF. GIVE IT BACK!
GO ON! BEAT IT, BRATS!
THANKS . . . AU REVOIR, MADAME.
PHEW! LET'S FIND THE SEA AGAIN AND ORIENT OURSELVES. IT MUST BE ABOUT TIME FOR THE MOVIE.
52

THERE'S STILL PLENTY OF TIME BEFORE WE LEAVE. WHAT SHOULD WE DO?
THE SAME FILM THREE TIMES IN A ROW, THAT WAS A BIT MUCH! AND IT'S FOUR O'CLOCK ALREADY.
YEAH, BUT IT WAS GREAT! NOW MY TUMMY IS GROWLING AND I HAVE A HEADACHE. HOW ABOUT A PASTRY?
WE COULD GO LOOK AT THE SEA AGAIN. FOR A WHILE.
THAT'S AFRICA OVER THERE.
HOW 'BOUT MENTON? WHERE'S THAT?
OVER THERE, BY ITALY.
FINDING OUR BROTHERS SHOULD BE EASY. I HAVE THEIR ADDRESS, AND THERE CAN'T BE THAT MANY BARBERSHOPS.

?
'SCUSE ME.
HEY! YOU! WHERE ARE YOU GOING?
JUST HEADING TO THE TRAIN.
WE FIGURED THAT. WHERE ARE YOUR PAPERS?
UH . . . MY DAD HAS THEM.
WHERE'S HE?

OVER THERE. TAKING CARE OF THE LUGGAGE.
WHERE DO YOU LIVE?
HERE IN MARSEILLE.
WHAT'S YOUR ADDRESS?
WE'RE ON CANEBIÈRE, OVER THE MOVIE THEATER.
MY DAD OWNS THE MOVIE THEATER.
YOU GO THERE A LOT?
YEAH! I SEE EVERY NEW MOVIE. RIGHT NOW IT'S BARON MUNCHAUSEN. IT'S GREAT!
ALL RIGHT. GET GOING.
MERCI! AU REVOIR, MESSIEURS!
?!

BONJOUR, MONSIEUR! DO YOU HAVE THE TIME?
?!

CAN'T YOU READ A CLOCK?

OF COURSE I CAN!
THEN JUST LOOK UP! THERE'S A CLOCK THAT'LL TELL YOU JUST AS WELL AS I CAN!

OH, RIGHT! THANKS, MONSIEUR!

?!

THEY'RE GONE. C'MON.

I HEARD PEOPLE TALKING. THE POLICE ARE CHECKING PAPERS ALL OVER THE STATION. LOTS OF PEOPLE GOT ARRESTED.
WHAT SHOULD WE DO?
IF WE LEAVE THE STATION, WE LOSE OUR TICKETS. THEY'RE ONLY GOOD FOR TONIGHT.
WHERE WOULD WE SLEEP IF WE STAY? THE HOTELS CHECK YOUR PAPERS TOO.
LOOK! BEHIND YOU.
DAMN.
IT'S A RAID!
LISTEN, IF WE FOLLOW THE TRACKS, WE COULD WALK TO ANOTHER STATION. RIGHT?
NO, WE COULD GET RUN OVER. BESIDES, THERE ARE GUYS WHO WORK THERE, GUARDING THE TRACKS. WE'D GET SPOTTED EVEN FASTER.
THE TRAIN FOR ITALY, VIA MENTON, IS NOW ENTERING TRACK 5.
THAT'S US! C'MON, RUN FOR IT!
57

WE JOINED IN THE STAMPEDE AND CHARGED TO THE FRONT.
FOR A MINUTE, IT WAS TOTAL CHAOS. THE FEW TRAINS COMING THROUGH WERE ALL OVERBOOKED.
BUT LUCK WAS WITH US. THE TICKET INSPECTORS HADN'T LOCKED THE DOORS, AND WE CLIMBED IN.
AFTER MORE THAN HALF AN HOUR'S DELAY, THE TRAIN LURCHED TO LIFE, AND WE LET OUT A HUGE SIGH OF RELIEF. WE WERE ON THE LAST LEG OF OUR JOURNEY.
58

WE HAD A LONG TRIP ON THE LOCAL TRAIN.
IT OFTEN STOPPED IN THE MIDDLE OF NOWHERE. WORKERS WALKED ON THE TRACKS, AND HALF-ASLEEP, I HEARD THEIR VOICES, THEIR ACCENTS, THEIR CURSES.

DAWN BROKE NEAR CANNES, AND SOON AFTER, THE TRAIN ARRIVED IN MENTON.

I DON'T REALLY KNOW HOW . . .
MENTON
. . . BUT I FOUND MYSELF IN A SQUARE WITH PALM TREES WAVING THEIR FRONDS ABOVE MY HEAD.
THEY WERE THE FIRST I'D EVER SEEN.
END OF PART ONE
60

part two

WE'VE BEEN IN MENTON FOR TWO WEEKS NOW.
RIGHT FROM THE START, THIS LITTLE TOWN, RINGED BY MOUNTAINS PLUNGING INTO THE MEDITERRANEAN, HAD CAST A SPELL OVER ME, WITH ITS ARCADES, ITS OLD CHURCHES, AND FLIGHTS OF STAIRS.
ITALIAN OCCUPATION TROOPS COULD ALWAYS BE FOUND LAZING AROUND TOWN.
COIFF
COIFFEUR
OUR BIG BROTHERS HAD DONE WELL FOR THEMSELVES, TO SAY THE LEAST.
THEY WORKED AT A BARBERSHOP AND EARNED A GOOD LIVING.

. . . ENDLESS GAMES OF SOCCER ON THE BEACH, AND BOUNDLESS WANDERING ALONG STREETS AND PATHWAYS.

UP AND AT 'EM, CITY SLICKERS! YOUR COUNTRY BROTHER'S HERE, AND HE ISN'T EMPTY-HANDED!
?!
WHAT'S THE MATTER?
WHY THE LONG FACES?
WE GOT SOME BAD NEWS.
MAMA AND PAPA?
MIGHT AS WELL TELL YOU UP FRONT. THEY WERE ARRESTED.
HOW DID IT HAPPEN?
THEY LEFT PARIS AFTER A MASSIVE ROUNDUP AND MADE IT TO THE FREE ZONE, BUT THE VICHY AUTHORITIES CAUGHT THEM THERE AND PUT THEM IN A CAMP.
THEY MANAGED TO GET THIS LETTER THROUGH. THAT'S HOW WE FOUND OUT.

. . . LOCKED UP IN A CAMP. IF YOU MEET UP WITH THE LITTLE HOOLIGANS, PUT THEM IN SCHOOL. IT'S VERY IMPORTANT. I'M COUNTING ON YOU. I KISS YOU ALL. BE BRAVE. PAPA AND MAMA
SO WHAT DO WE DO NOW?
WELL, I GUESS I'M GOING THERE.
BUT IF YOU GO, THEY'LL KNOW YOU'RE JEWISH! THEY'LL LOCK YOU UP TOO!
THAT'S WHAT I SAID YESTERDAY TOO. BUT WE'VE BEEN UP ALL NIGHT TALKING AND WE FINALLY AGREED ON ONE THING: WE HAVE TO TRY SOMETHING.
I'LL BE BACK AS SOON AS I CAN. ALBERT WILL ENROLL YOU IN SCHOOL THIS AFTERNOON. WORKING IS ALL WELL AND GOOD, BUT PAPA'S RIGHT.
SCHOOL IS VERY IMPORTANT, RIGHT?
RIGHT . . .

REALLY, IT'S QUITE BOTHERSOME, NOT HAVING THEIR PAPERS. IN THEORY, I'M NOT ALLOWED TO LET THEM ENROLL.
BUT WE CAN'T VERY WELL DEPRIVE THEM OF AN EDUCATION, CAN WE?
SO IT'S SETTLED, THEN! I'LL SHOW THEM TO THEIR CLASSROOMS.
RIGHT NOW?
OF COURSE. WHEN ELSE?
IF YOU PLEASE, SIR, I'LL BRING THEM BACK TOMORROW MORNING. THEY STILL NEED SATCHELS AND NOTEBOOKS.
TRUE, TRUE. AND DON'T FORGET SLATES AND CHALK. THOSE WILL BE USEFUL. THE SCHOOL WILL SUPPLY THE BOOKS.
"DAWN," BY ARTHUR RIMBAUD. "I HAVE KISSED THE SUMMER DAWN. BEFORE THE PALACES, NOTHING MOVED."

WHAT A STINKER! DID YOU SEE HOW HE WANTED TO YANK US IN RIGHT AWAY, BEFORE WE EVEN HAD TIME TO CATCH OUR BREATH?
YOU BETTER STAY ON THE STRAIGHT AND NARROW AROUND HIM. I'M SURE HE'S GOT AN EYE ON YOU ALREADY!
SCHOOL TOMORROW! G'NIGHT, YOU RASCALS!

CLIC
?!
MAMA AND PAPA ARE FREE.
WE LISTENED AS HENRI TOLD HIS TALE, HANGING ON HIS EVERY WORD. IT WAS WORTHY OF THE HEROIC EXPLOITS OF GRANDFATHER JOFFO.

AT THE CAMP IN PAU, HENRI GOT OFF ON THE WRONG FOOT.
BUT THERE'S BEEN A MISTAKE! SERGEANT, I SWEAR MY PARENTS AREN'T JEWS!
THERE MUST BE SOME WAY WE CAN REACH AN UNDERSTANDING!
YOU HAVE TO GET IN AND SEE THE COMMANDANT. BUT I'M TELLING YOU . . .
UNLESS YOU HAVE CONNECTIONS, HE WON'T SEE YOU.
OF COURSE. BUT WE'RE ORDINARY PEOPLE. WE'VE NEVER BEEN INVOLVED IN POLITICS. MY FATHER WAS JUST COMING TO HELP ME OUT AT THE BARBERSHOP WHERE I WORK.
YOU'RE A BARBER? SAY, MAYBE WE CAN WORK SOMETHING OUT AFTER ALL!
COULD YOU GIVE ME A LITTLE TRIM? I DON'T HAVE TIME TO GO INTO PAU, AND THE CAPTAIN'S REAL HARD ON LONG HAIR.
I COULD GET MY LEAVE REVOKED.
I'LL SEE WHAT I CAN DO ABOUT YOUR PARENTS. NO PROMISES, EH?
AND SO WITH A RAZOR BORROWED FROM THE OWNER AND WATER FROM THE COFFEEMAKER, HENRI GAVE HIM THE BEST HAIRCUT OF HIS LIFE.
THEN HENRI SPENT THE NIGHT WAITING IN A ROOM OF A FLEABAG HOTEL.

THE NEXT MORNING, HE SHOWED UP AT THE SENTRY BOX.
MICHAUD. SERGEANT MICHAUD. HE TOLD ME TO COME HERE AT TEN O'CLOCK.
I DON'T WANT TO HEAR IT! CIVILIANS AREN'T ALLOWED TO LOITER OUTSIDE THE GATES. BEAT IT!
BONNART! IT'S OK! LET HIM IN. I'LL TAKE CARE OF IT.
SORRY, BUT WE HAVE TO BE REAL STRICT WITH SECURITY.
I UNDERSTAND...
HE'LL SEE YOU ALL RIGHT, BUT BE CAREFUL. HE'S GROUCHY TODAY.
HE USUALLY IS, BUT TODAY HE'S EVEN WORSE. HERE WE ARE. GOOD LUCK.
OFFICE
THANK YOU SO MUCH, SERGEANT.
KNOCK KNOCK
COME IN!

SIT DOWN.
HENRI JOFFO. MAKE IT SHORT. IN COMING HERE, YOU'RE RISKING YOUR FREEDOM WITHOUT ANY GUARANTEE OF FREEING YOUR PARENTS.
WE'RE UNDER ORDERS TO HAND OVER ALL FOREIGN JEWS TO THE OCCUPATION AUTHORITIES.

NOW, I'VE GOT 600 SUSPECTS HERE. IF I LET EVEN ONE GO WITHOUT A VALID REASON, I MIGHT AS WELL RELEASE THE REST.

MONSIEUR COMMANDANT, I'M FRENCH. I WAS AT DUNKIRK AND THE BELGIAN CAMPAIGN.
I'M NOT HERE TO BEG FAVORS BUT TO TELL YOU THERE'S BEEN A MISTAKE. NO ONE IN MY FAMILY IS JEWISH.
WHAT PROOF DO YOU HAVE?

FIRST OF ALL, MY MOTHER'S CATHOLIC. YOU HAVE HER FAMILY REGISTER. HER MAIDEN NAME IS MARKOFF. I CHALLENGE ANYONE TO FIND A SINGLE JEW NAMED MARKOFF.

IN FACT, WE'RE DESCENDED FROM THE JUNIOR BRANCH OF THE ROMANOFFS—THE RUSSIAN ROYAL FAMILY.
THERE'S NO WAY A MEMBER OF THE ROYAL FAMILY COULD HAVE BEEN JEWISH. THAT WOULD'VE BROUGHT THE RUSSIAN ORTHODOX CHURCH TUMBLING DOWN!

AND YOUR FATHER?

ALL JEWS WERE STRIPPED OF THEIR CITIZENSHIP BY THE GERMANS. BUT AS HIS PAPERS ATTEST, MY FATHER'S FRENCH.
IF HE'S FRENCH, HE'S NOT JEWISH. THERE'S NO IN-BETWEEN.

IF YOU WANT TO BE ABSOLUTELY SURE, YOU CAN CALL THE PREFECTURE IN PARIS.
GET ME POLICE HEADQUARTERS IN PARIS. IDENTITY VERIFICATION DEPARTMENT.
HELLO, IDENTITY VERIFICATION DEPARTMENT?
I NEED SOME INFORMATION ABOUT SOMEONE NAMED JOFFO RESIDING ON THE RUE CLIGNANCOURT. PROFESSION: BARBER. HAS HE BEEN STRIPPED OF FRENCH CITIZENSHIP?
THAT'S RIGHT, JOFFO. 12 RUE CLIGNANCOURT.
FINE, THANKS. VERY GOOD.
YOUR FATHER IS IN FACT STILL A FRENCH CITIZEN. I'LL HAVE HIM FREED, ALONG WITH YOUR MOTHER.

HALF AN HOUR LATER, THE THREE OF THEM WERE REUNITED. THEY HOPPED ON THE FIRST BUS TO GET AWAY AS QUICKLY AS THEY COULD.
BUT WHERE ARE THEY NOW?
IN NICE. WE'LL GO SEE THEM ONCE THEY'RE SAFELY SETTLED IN.
HOW COME THE GUY AT THE PREFECTURE SAID OUR PARENTS WEREN'T JEWISH?
WHO KNOWS? MAYBE THE PAPERWORK HADN'T GONE THROUGH YET. A DELAY, AN OVERSIGHT. IT HAPPENS. OR MAYBE THE GUY JUST SAID WHATEVER HE FELT LIKE BECAUSE HE COULDN'T FIND THE FILE.
OR MAYBE THE COMMANDANT LIED.
MAYBE HE FOUND OUT PAPA WAS JEWISH BUT PRETENDED NOT TO SO HE COULD FREE THEM!
I DON'T KNOW. HE SEEMED REALLY STRICT, BUT...
IT COULD BE. YOU NEVER REALLY KNOW.
YES, A HERO WHO HID HIS GENEROSITY UNDER A STERN MASK. THAT WAS BETTER THAN SOME PENCIL PUSHER'S OVERSIGHT. I WAS SURE THAT WAS HOW MY PARENTS WERE SAVED.
SINCE THEN, I'VE COME TO THINK OTHERWISE.

SO WHO HAS THE BEST-LOOKING SWIMSUIT?
YOO-HOO!
I DO, WHO ELSE?
BESIDES, IT'S NOT LIKE THAT SUIT'LL MAKE YOU FASTER IN THE WATER.
OH YEAH? WELL, WE'LL SEE TOMORROW AT THE BEACH. I'LL WHIP YOU IN THE 25-METER.
KNOCK KNOCK
MUST BE MY BUDDIES LOOKING TO PLAY POOL. HURRY UP WITH THE DISHES, MAURICE.
OK, OK! IT'S NOT LIKE EVERYONE ELSE IS READY.
BONJOUR. DO ALBERT AND HENRI JOFFO LIVE HERE?
?!
I'M ALBERT. BUT MY BROTHER'S OUT. WHAT'S THIS ABOUT?
THESE ARE TWO SUMMONS. YOU BOTH MUST REPORT TO THE PREFECTURE WITHIN TWO DAYS. IT'S FOR THE CWS.

EVERYBODY'S BEING TAKEN, YOU KNOW. WE JUST BRING THE ORDERS. WE DON'T WRITE THEM.
I SEE.
SURE. OF COURSE, OF COURSE.
THAT'S ALL. DON'T FORGET: YOU HAVE TWO DAYS.
GOT IT. AU REVOIR!
WHAT'S THE CWS?
COMPULSORY WORK SERVICE. IT MEANS WE HAVE TO GO TO GERMANY AND CUT KRAUT HAIR. AT LEAST THAT'S WHAT THEY THINK.
YEAH, NO WAY WE'RE WALKING RIGHT INTO THE LION'S DEN! SO THAT'S IT, THEN—WE'RE LEAVING.
WHEN?
TOMORROW MORNING. WE PACK AS FAST AS WE CAN AND LEAVE AT DAWN. NO POINT HANGING AROUND.
WHERE WILL WE GO?
YOU'LL LIKE THIS, JO: WE'RE GOING TO NICE!

IN NICE IT WAS SUMMER . . .
MARCELLO! MARCELLO!

HELLO, BAMBINO!

THE TOMATOES, GIVE THEM.
THANKS, MARCELLO! EIGHT POUNDS A BAG IS HEAVY!

THIS WAY, WE'LL GO TO TITO'S.
THERE YOU GO, FELLAS!
BUONGIORNO!
HELLO, JO!

A LITTLE LESS OLIVE OIL FOR US AND A LITTLE MORE FOR FRANCE!
YOU GET THIS MUCH EVERY DAY?
WE GET IT BY THE LITER! AND THAT'S NOT COUNTING CANNED FOOD: TUNA IN OIL, SARDINES IN OIL . . .
BUT NEVER ANYTHING FRESH LIKE THESE TOMATOES! WHAT WE NEED TO GO WITH THEM ARE SOME FRESH GREEN HERBS . . .
PARSLEY?
THAT'S IT! PARSLEY!
THE BUTCHER BY THE DOCKS SHOULD HAVE SOME. HE'S A SMOKER.
WE'LL NEED SOME CIGARETTES.
SO THE TRUCK FARMER GIVES US TOMATOES AND SOME CASH FOR ITALIAN OLIVE OIL. WITH THE CASH AND PACKS OF CIGARETTES CARLO SLIPS US, WE CAN BUY BLACK-MARKET RICE.
MAYBE WE COULD HAGGLE DOWN THE PRICE OF RICE AND KEEP A FEW CIGARETTES TO GET PARSLEY FROM THE BUTCHER.
WITH THE RICE, WE CAN GET SACKS OF FLOUR FOR MAMA ROSSO, WHICH THE ITALIANS USE TO MAKE PASTA.
pâtes
maraîcher
riz
TITE
WE GET SOME, PLUS THE MONEY FROM THE TOMATOES, AND VOILÀ!
16

HA HA! OK, SEE YOU LATER!

YOOHOO!
OH, IT'S YOU, JO.
GO WASH YOUR HANDS BEFORE DINNER. WHERE'S MAURICE?
UH . . . SORRY I'M LATE, MAMAN.
?
HE WON'T BE LONG. HE WENT TO THE HARDWARE STORE FOR SOME SHAVING CREAM.
YOU TWO AND YOUR SCHEMES!
SPEAK OF THE DEVIL!
DON'T FORGET, WE'RE LIVING IN AN OCCUPIED COUNTRY.
THOSE ITALIANS MIGHT BE NICE, BUT THE DAY MAY COME WHEN—
AH, WE KNOW ALL THE ITALIANS!
HAVEN'T YOU HEARD? THESE TWO ARE GOING TO BUY THE HOTEL NEGRESCO! THE FUNNY PART IS, SOMETIMES I WONDER IF THEY WON'T ACTUALLY SUCCEED!
18

HURRY UP AND EAT, JO. NO TIME TO HANG AROUND.
WHERE TO NOW?
WELL, THE HARDWARE STORE'S OUT OF SHAVING CREAM. BUT HE CAN GET SOME MORE BY RESOLING LEATHER SHOES. SO WE HAVE TO SEE THE COBBLER ON RUE SAINT-PIERRE AND TRADE—
SPEAKING OF COBBLERS, LET ME TELL YOU A STORY.
DES DÉBATS
ET LITTÉRAIRES
ONE MAN SAYS TO ANOTHER: THERE'S A VERY EASY WAY FOR ALL MEN TO LIVE TOGETHER IN PEACE. JUST KILL ALL THE JEWS AND THE COBBLERS.
THE OTHER LOOKS AT HIM IN ASTONISHMENT. AFTER A MOMENT OF REFLECTION, HE ASKS: WHY KILL THE COBBLERS?
BUT... WHY THE JEWS?
THAT'S EXACTLY THE QUESTION THAT FAILED TO SPRING TO THE MAN'S MIND.
AND THAT'S WHY IT'S A FUNNY STORY.
YES, IN NICE IT WAS SUMMER, AND THE WAR DEFINITELY FELT FAR AWAY.

* CITIZENS, TO ARMS! FORM YOUR BATTALIONS!
** MARCH ON! MARCH ON!

BUT A MOTHER'S BIRTHDAY IS PRICELESS . . .
THANK YOU, DARLINGS. YOU'VE REALLY OUTDONE YOURSELVES!
IMAGINE THAT—JEWELS FROM THE YOUNGER BOYS, A SEWING MACHINE FROM THE OLDER ONES . . .
WE NEEDED GIFTS WORTHY OF A ROMANOFF!
NOW, YOUR
SPOILED! I MAD
CAKE. IT'S NOT MISSING A SINGLE ALMOND!
YUMMM!
I'LL JUST HAVE A BITE. IT'S TIME FOR THE BRITISH BROADCAST.
TELL US THE NEWS! I CAN'T BRING MYSELF TO LEAVE DESSERT!
OK, BUT SAVE ME SOME! I NEVER SAID I'D SACRIFICE IT ON THE ALTAR OF CURRENT EVENTS.
SPEAKING OF WHICH, I HAD A CUSTOMER WHOSE HUSBAND WORKS FOR THE VICHY NEWS SERVICE. SHE CONFIRMED THAT THE KRAUTS TOOK A BEATING IN STALINGRAD!
THEY MIGHT EVEN BE CLOSE TO—
THE ALLIES HAVE LANDED IN NORTH AFRICA! ALGERIA AND MOROCCO!
HAPPY BIRTHDAY, DARLING!

L'EUROPE
MEDITERRA
ALGER
MAROC
Kama
VOLGA
Don
Stalingrad
Kharkof
Tunis
Sus
Palerme
Mess
Etna
Sicile
E R
Malte
chez TIT

HELLO, MARCELLO! I . . . I'M HERE FOR YOUR FRENCH LESSON.
SALUT, JO! I DIDN'T SEE YOU. SIT DOWN. I'LL BUY YOU A GRENADINE.
BUT DON'T BOTHER WITH THE FRENCH LESSON. I WON'T HAVE TIME ANYMORE.
I HAVE TO LEAVE SOON.
YOUR REGIMENT GOT TRANSFERRED?
NO, WE'RE ALL LEAVING. ALL THE ITALIANS.
MUSSOLINI'S NOT IN CHARGE ANYMORE. BADOGLIO IS, AND HE'S MAKING PEACE WITH THE ALLIES. SO WE'RE GOING HOME, MAYBE EVEN TO WAR WITH HITLER NOW!
BUT IF YOU'RE LEAVING, THEN WE'RE FREE!
NO. IF WE LEAVE, THEN THE GERMANS WILL COME.
SEPTEMBER 10, 1943 NICE TRAIN STATION . . .
23

DING
DING
DING
DING
MICHEL STROGOFF
VOYAGES
DING
DING
DING
DING
DING
DING
DING
DING
DING
DING
DING
WHAT ARE YOUR BROTHERS UP TO? IT'S SIX ALREADY!
AH, THERE YOU ARE! WE WERE STARTING TO GET WORRIED!
24

WELL?

WELL, IT'S SIMPLE. WE HAVE TO LEAVE RIGHT AWAY.

THE GERMANS ARE ARRESTING ALL THE JEWS AND LOCKING THEM UP IN THE HOTEL EXCELSIOR. THEN SPECIAL TRAINS TAKE THEM AWAY AT NIGHT.

IN SHORT, STAYING HERE IS BUYING A ONE-WAY TICKET TO GERMANY.

WELL, CHILDREN, HENRI'S RIGHT. WE'LL HAVE TO SPLIT UP AGAIN.

I'VE HAD TIME TO THINK THESE LAST FEW DAYS. WE'LL STICK WITH THE METHOD THAT'S WORKED WELL BEFORE AND GO IN TWOS.

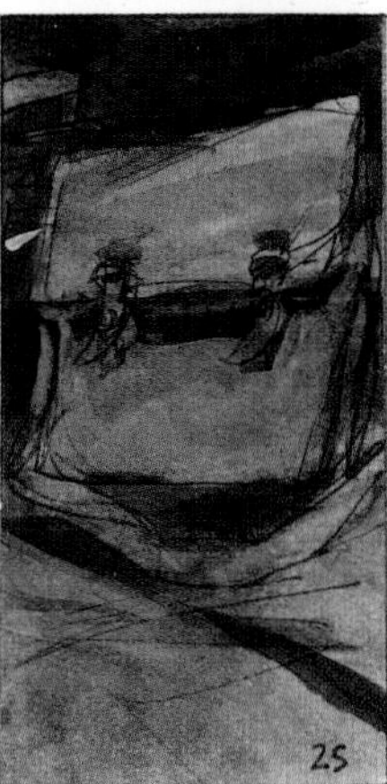

MOISSON NOUVELLE
SO ARE WE GOING IN?
WE'RE GOING IN. A VICHY CAMP IS THE LAST PLACE NAZIS WOULD COME LOOKING FOR TWO JEWISH BOYS.
ARE YOU NEW? WHO SENT YOU?
CLAC
UH . . . WE WANT TO SEE THE DIRECTOR, MONSIEUR SUBINAGUI.
CLAC
FOLLOW ME.

TWO NEW BOYS TO SEE YOU, MONSIEUR DIRECTOR.
THANK YOU, GERARD. LEAVE US.
CLAC
DON'T BE ALARMED. GERARD'S FATHER WAS AN ARMY SERGEANT AND RAISED HIM IN A VERY... SPECIAL ATMOSPHERE.
BUT HE'S QUITE NICE.
YOUR FATHER TOLD ME ABOUT YOU. YOU'LL BE FINE HERE, AND... SAFE.
I'M QUITE BUSY, SO I'LL BE BRIEF. YOU CAN STAY IN CAMP AND SEE TO DAILY OPERATIONS, KITCHEN DUTY, AND CLEANING.
OR YOU CAN WORK AT OUR POTTERY WORKSHOP IN VALLAURIS. OUR COMMUNITY MAKES A LIVING OFF THE PRODUCTS WE SELL. YOU'LL GET WAGES, OF COURSE.
IT'S UP TO YOU. YOU CAN PICK TOMORROW. FOR NOW, CATCH UP WITH GERARD. HE'LL SHOW YOU WHERE TO SETTLE IN.

CLAC
FOLLOW ME!

HERE WE ARE. YOUR BUNKS ARE IN THE BACK.
SUPPER'S AT SIX, WE LOWER THE FLAG AT SEVEN, SHOWER AT EIGHT THIRTY, AND IN YOUR BUNKS BY NINE. LIGHTS OUT AT NINE FIFTEEN.
DON'T WORRY. HE'S A LITTLE CRACKED, BUT HE'S A GOOD GUY.
?
I'M ANGE TESTI. I MANAGED TO DUCK OUT OF KITCHEN DUTY TODAY BY SAYING MY STOMACH HURT.
GOTTA SNEAK A NAP IN, TO GET THROUGH THE DAY.
SO... IS IT NICE HERE?
YEAH, IT'S GREAT!
THERE ARE A LOT OF JEWS.
YOU TOO?
UH... NO. ARE YOU A JEW?
HA HA!
NOT A CHANCE. BAPTIZED, HOLY COMMUNION, CONFIRMATION, AND A CHOIRBOY TO BOOT!
HOW'D YOU WIND UP HERE?
28

WELL, I'M ON VACATION, YOU SEE.
I'LL EXPLAIN. BUT I'M GONNA HIDE DOWN HERE, IF YOU DON'T MIND. IF THE KITCHEN GUY CATCHES ME GOOFING OFF, HE'S NOT GOING TO BE TOO HAPPY!
I'M ORIGINALLY FROM ALGERIA: RIGHT FROM BAB EL-OUED!
I WANTED TO SEE FRANCE. I'D NEVER BEEN BEFORE. MY FATHER SAID OK, SO DURING ALL SAINTS' DAY, I WENT AND STAYED WITH A COUSIN IN PARIS.
THERE I WAS, STROLLING DOWN THE CHAMPS-ÉLYSÉES WHEN THE AMERICANS LANDED IN NORTH AFRICA! NO CHANCE OF GOING HOME BEFORE THE WAR WAS OVER.
Le Petit Parisien
MOISSON NOUVELLE
TO TOP IT ALL OFF, MY COUSIN FOUND A GIRL AND THREW ME OUT! I HEADED SOUTH FOR THE WARM WEATHER, WITHOUT A PENNY TO MY NAME. AFTER A LITTLE PANHANDLING, I WOUND UP HERE. SUBINAGUI AGREED TO TAKE ME IN.
IT'S EASIER THAN SELLING SHOES ALL DAY IN MY FATHER'S SHOP IN ALGERIA.
IMAGINE: IF THE WAR LASTS TEN YEARS, I'LL HAVE HAD A TEN-YEAR VACATION!
HOW MANY KIDS ARE IN THE CAMP?
OH, ABOUT A HUNDRED. SOME COME, SOME GO. IT DOESN'T CHANGE MUCH, BUT IT'S A NICE PLACE. YOU'LL SEE.
CLANG CLANG
AH! SUPPERTIME! NOT A MINUTE TOO SOON!
C'MON, ALL THE GOOD STUFF GETS SNAPPED UP FAST!

APART FROM A FEW DOWNSIDES HERE AND THERE, THAT WAS THE START OF THREE WONDERFUL WEEKS . . .

MAURICE?
HNNH?

I HEARD SUBINAGUI TALKING TO THE COOK. SOUNDS LIKE THE NAZIS HAVE STEPPED UP THE HUNT FOR JEWS. EVERYONE SUSPECTED OF BEING JEWISH IS BEING SHIPPED STRAIGHT TO GERMAN CAMPS.

I KNOW. AND IF THE KRAUTS RAID THIS PLACE, I THINK THEY'LL KNOW WE'RE JEWISH RIGHT AWAY.

HOW? UP TILL NOW—

THE GESTAPO DOESN'T EVEN BOTHER ASKING ANYMORE. OUR NAME IS JOFFO, AND WE COME FROM THE JEWISH QUARTER IN PARIS? THAT'S ENOUGH FOR THEM!

SO WE HAVE TO MAKE SOMETHING UP. REMEMBER ANGE'S STORY? WELL, SAME WITH US. WE CAME TO FRANCE ON VACATION AND GOT STUCK BECAUSE OF THE ALLIED LANDING.
THEY WON'T BE ABLE TO CHECK OUT OUR STORY. NO WAY TO CONTACT OUR FRIENDS OR PARENTS.

SO WHERE ARE WE FROM?
ALGIERS.
AND WHAT DID OUR PARENTS DO?
PAPA CUTS HAIR. MAMA DOESN'T WORK.
AND WHERE DO WE LIVE?
10 RUE JEAN-JAURÈS.

WHY 10 RUE JEAN-JAURÈS?

BECAUSE THERE'S A RUE JEAN-JAURÈS IN EVERY TOWN, AND 10 IS EASY TO REMEMBER.

IF THEY ASK ABOUT OUR HOUSE OR THE STORE, JUST DESCRIBE RUE CLIGNANCOURT. THAT WAY WE WON'T MESS ANYTHING UP.

C'MON, DON'T WORRY. GET SOME SLEEP. WE'RE NOT ALONE HERE, AND SUBINAGUI WILL HELP US.
COMPAGNONS DE FRANCE
THERE'LL ALWAYS BE SOMEONE TO HELP US.
31

LOOK AT THAT! WE'RE SO LUCKY FERDINAND SAID WE COULD COME ALONG ON HIS GROCERY RUN! NOW WE'LL GET TO SEE OUR PARENTS!
YOU GOT ANY PLANS?
NO! WE'RE JUST GOING TO WALK AROUND.
HEY, JOFFOS! THERE'S NICE! HELLOOOO!
OK. I GOTTA STOP ON RUE DE RUSSIE, SEE A PAL REAL QUICK.
AFTER THAT, I'LL SHOW YOU WHERE THE BUS STATION IS SO YOU DON'T MISS YOUR RIDE HOME TONIGHT.
THEN YOU'RE FREE!
IT'S OVER HERE.
JUST WAIT. I'LL BE BACK IN A MINUTE.
32

G.F.P. Luftw.
O.Qu.West
Zahnstation
WHAT'S HE UP TO?
HE'S BEEN GONE MAYBE TWO MINUTES.
ARE YOU NUTS? IT'S BEEN AT LEAST TEN!
HOW CAN YOU TELL IT'S BEEN TEN? DO YOU HAVE A WATCH?
I DON'T NEED A WATCH! I CAN TELL. IF YOU CAN'T TELL THE DIFFERENCE BETWEEN TWO MINUTES AND HALF AN HOUR, YOU MIGHT AS WELL JUMP OFF THE NEAREST DOCK.
WHATEVER, STUPID . . .

WELL I'VE HAD IT. I'M GOING LOOKING FOR HIM. WE CAN FIND THE STATION BY OURSELVES ANYWAY, AND I WON'T SPEND THE WHOLE AFTERNOON COOLING MY HEELS.

JUST WAIT HERE FOR ME. I'LL BE RIGHT BACK.

JEEZ, WHAT ARE THOSE JERKS UP TO?
IF THIS IS SOME TRICK, I'M GONNA . . .
OK, I'M COUNTING MY STEPS TO THE DOOR, AND IF THEY'RE NOT BACK BY THEN, I'M GOING BACK TO CAMP. THEY CAN JUST STUFF IT.

1...2...3...
17...18...19...
33...34...35...
36!
MAURICE? FERDINAND?
MAURICE?
35

KIKE.
AAAAH!
KIKE!
36

WHY ME? I'D GIVE ANYTHING FOR THOSE PAPERS. AND JUST WHEN IT LOOKED LIKE THINGS WOULD BE ALL RIGHT...

POOF...

WHAT TIME IS IT?
QUARTER AFTER FIVE.
ALREADY? WE'VE BEEN HERE FOR MORE THAN THREE HOURS! WHAT ARE THEY DOING?
MAYBE THEY FORGOT US? THEY MUST BE LOOKING FOR THE RÉSISTANCE LEADERS. WE'RE WORTHLESS TO THEM.
I WOULDN'T BET ON IT, BROTHER. BUT ONCE THEY'VE QUESTIONED US, THEY'LL REALIZE THEIR MISTAKE. AT LEAST I HOPE SO . . .
OR ELSE WHAT? THEY'VE NABBED US ALL. WHAT A HAUL! NOW THAT THEY'VE GOT US, THEY'LL PROBABLY GO ON AND WIN THE WAR!
WHAT DID WE EVER DO TO THEM? THAT SOLDIER, THE WAY HE LOOKED AT ME . . . IT WAS LIKE ALL HE'D EVER DREAMED OF WAS SMASHING ME AGAINST THE WALL.
THIS IS RIDICULOUS. I'M ELEVEN YEARS OLD. I DON'T KNOW ANY GERMANS. HOW CAN I BE THEIR ENEMY?
OUTSIDE! SCHNELL! SCHNELL! *

* QUICKLY!

GET IN!
SCHNELL!

* I'M BRINGING THESE THREE UPSTAIRS TO START WITH. YOU GUYS WAIT HERE WITH THE KIDS. I'LL LET YOU KNOW.
** YES, SIR!

* YOU, THERE! IT'S YOUR TURN! BRING THEM UP!.
** GO RIGHT IN, THE BOTH OF YOU!

YOUR TURN NOW. YOU ARE BROTHERS?
YES. HE'S JOSEPH, AND I'M MAURICE.
JOSEPH AND MAURICE WHAT?
JOFFO.
. . . AND YOU'RE JEWS.
NO, WE'RE NOT!
WE'RE NOT JEWS, WE'RE FROM ALGERIA. WE WERE ON VACATION IN FRANCE AND GOT STUCK BECAUSE OF THE LANDING.
WHAT WERE YOU DOING ON RUE DE RUSSIE?
WE CAME FROM THE COMPAGNONS DE FRANCE CAMP. FERDINAND TOOK US ON HIS GROCERY RUN, AND WE WERE WAITING FOR HIM LIKE HE TOLD US TO, WHILE HE WENT TO SEE A FRIEND. NO ONE KNEW HE WAS A JEW.
AND YOU'RE CATHOLIC?
OF COURSE.
YOU'VE BEEN BAPTIZED?
YES, AND WE'VE TAKEN COMMUNION.
WHICH CHURCH?
LA BUFFA, IN NICE.
WHY NOT ALGIERS?
MAMAN LIKED FRANCE BETTER. SHE ALSO HAD A COUSIN AROUND HERE.

VERY WELL, WE WILL VERIFY ALL THIS. FOR NOW, YOU WILL UNDERGO A PHYSICAL EXAMINATION, TO SEE IF YOU'RE CIRCUMCISED.

* THIS WAS PERFORMED FOR SURGICAL REASONS.

WELL.
WE CHECKED, AND THE HEAD OF MOISSON NOUVELLE CONFIRMED EVERY DETAIL OF YOUR STORY.
YOU, THE OLDER ONE—GET OUT OF HERE. YOU HAVE ONE WEEK TO BRING US PROOF THAT YOU'RE NOT JEWISH. WE NEED COMMUNION CERTIFICATES FROM THE PRIEST IN NICE. FIGURE IT OUT.
IF YOU DON'T COME BACK, WE'LL MAKE MINCEMEAT OF YOUR BROTHER.
A GUARD WILL LEAD YOU TO ONE OF THE ROOMS WE'RE USING AS CELLS.
BETTER HURRY.
LISTEN, MAURICE, IF YOU THINK YOU HAVE A CHANCE OF FREEING ME, THEN COME BACK. OTHERWISE, KEEP AWAY AND HIDE.
AT LEAST ONE OF US SHOULD STAY ALIVE.

DON'T WORRY. I'LL BE BACK IN A WEEK.
SALUT.

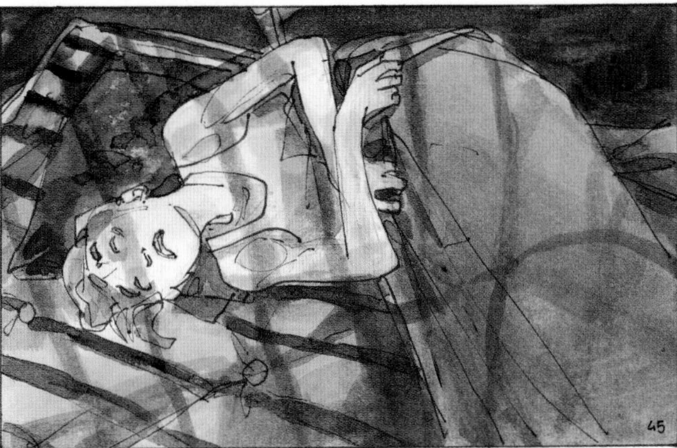
45

SOUNDS LIKE YOU THOUGHT I WOULDN'T BE!

I GOT THE PAPERS! C'MON GET UP AND GET DRESSED. TODAY WE'RE GETTING OUT OF HERE.

VERY WELL. EVERYTHING IS IN ORDER. YOU ARE FREE TO GO.
REALLY, I MUST SAY IT TOOK YOU LONG ENOUGH.
MAURICE, JOSEPH. SAY GOOD-BYE TO THE GENTLEMAN.
AU REVOIR, MONSIEUR!
HOTEL RUH

AU REVOIR, CHILDREN. BE GOOD, GOOD LUCK, AND GOD BLESS!
THANK YOU, FATHER!
AU REVOIR! THANKS AGAIN FOR EVERYTHING!
?
SAY, MONSIEUR SUBINAGUI . . . WHY ARE OUR BAGS BACK THERE?
WE'RE NOT GOING BACK TO THE CAMP. I'M TAKING YOU STRAIGHT TO THE STATION.
I PUT EVERYTHING YOU NEED IN YOUR KNAPSACKS: CLOTHES, A SNACK, TICKETS . . . YOU'LL TAKE THE TRAIN TO AIX-LES-BAINS, WHERE YOUR BROTHERS ARE WAITING.
WHAT'S GOING ON?
YOUR FATHER'S BEEN ARRESTED.
IF THE GERMANS TIE HIM TO YOU, THEY'LL COME TAKE YOU BACK. NO SENSE HANGING AROUND. YOU HAVE TO GET GOING RIGHT AWAY.
LUCKILY, YOUR MOTHER WAS WARNED IN TIME AND ESCAPED. I CAN'T SAY WHERE, BUT REST ASSURED, SHE'S SAFE.

I DIDN'T EVEN CRY. A YEAR AGO, I WOULDN'T HAVE BEEN ABLE TO BEAR THE THOUGHT THAT PAPA HAD BEEN ARRESTED. I'VE GROWN, HARDENED, CHANGED . . .

MY HEART HAS GROWN ACCUSTOMED TO DANGER AND DISASTER. MAYBE I CAN NO LONGER FEEL REAL SORROW. THE LOST CHILD I WAS EIGHTEEN MONTHS AGO WHEN WE LEFT PARIS HAS DWINDLED AWAY BIT BY BIT ON THE TRAINS, THE ROADS OF PROVENCE, THE HOTEL HALLWAYS IN NICE.
THE NAZIS HAVEN'T TAKEN MY LIFE AWAY YET, BUT THEY'VE STOLEN MY CHILDHOOD.

TOMORROW I'LL BE IN AIX-LES-BAINS. IF THAT DOESN'T WORK OUT, WE'LL GO SOMEWHERE ELSE, FARTHER, ANYWHERE. I DON'T CARE. MAYBE I DON'T REALLY CARE THAT MUCH ABOUT LIFE ANYMORE.
BUT THINGS ARE IN MOTION NOW, THE GAME WILL GO ON, AND RULES SAY THE HUNTED MUST ALWAYS RUN FROM THE HUNTER. WHILE I STILL HAVE MY WIND, I'LL DO ALL I CAN TO ROB THEM OF THE PLEASURE OF CATCHING ME.

THROUGH THE WINDOW, I WATCH THE SAD, FLAT FIELDS VANISH BIT BY BIT. IT SEEMS AS THOUGH I CAN ALREADY SEE THE PEAKS, THE SNOW, THE RED AUTUMN LEAVES. ALREADY THE FLOWERS AND FRAGRANCES OF THE MOUNTAINS ARE WASHING OVER ME . . .

LIBRAIRIE
MANCELIER
CHRISTMAS 1943, A VILLAGE NEAR AIX-LES-BAINS...
AH, MY DASHING MESSENGER! COME WARM YOURSELF BY THE FIRE, JO. DID YOU DELIVER ALL THE PAPERS?

YES, MONSIEUR MANCELIER. BUT IT'S GETTING HARDER TO BIKE AROUND. THERE'S LOTS OF ICE BEFORE DAWN, AND IT'S SLIPPERY!

YOU HAVE TO GET USED TO IT, MY BOY. A GREAT MAN IS DISTINGUISHED BY HIS ABILITY TO CONQUER THE WORST DIFFICULTIES!

YOU SEE, JOSEPH, THEY DON'T TEACH YOU THAT IN PUBLIC SCHOOL. AND THE SCHOOLS HAVE BECOME PUBLIC, TOO PUBLIC.
50

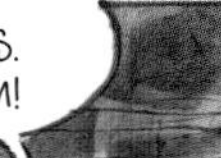

A BRIGHT, CLEAN EUROPE CAPABLE OF FENDING OFF ITS ENEMIES FROM THE EAST, WEST, AND SOUTH! HISTORICALLY, NOT MANY HAVE BEEN ABLE TO PULL IT OFF. HOW MANY?

HOW MANY ARE THERE, JOSEPH?

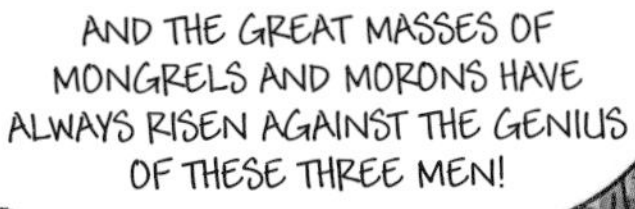

UH . . . FRANÇOISE? WH-WHATCHA DOIN'?
I'M GOING TO READ A LITTLE. WHY?
OH, NOTHING. I . . . I WAS JUST, I MEAN . . . I HAVE TO WRITE TO MY FAMILY AND AFTER THAT I—I WAS HEADED TO SEE MY BROTHER MAURICE AT THE HOTEL WHERE HE WORKS.
NEAT. HAVE FUN, JO!
TH—THANKS.
IF I SCRATCH OUT THIS #4 RATION STAMP . . . IT LOOKS LIKE A #1. NOW WE CAN GET SOME SUGAR! THAT'S THE MOST VALUABLE RATION.
JAL
JANVIER 1944
FÉVRIER 1944
MARS 1944
. . . AND SO, DEAR MAMAN, DON'T WORRY. THE MANCELIERS TREAT ME WELL AND ARE STILL TOTALLY IN THE DARK. MAURICE HAS A JOB AS A CLERK AT THE HOTEL DU COMMERCE, AND WE HAVE A FEW SCHEMES ON THE SIDE THAT MAKE LIFE EASIER. NOW THAT YOU'RE WITH OUR BROTHERS IN AIX, WE CAN SEE EACH OTHER SOMETIMES. GIVE THEM A KISS FOR ME. I NEED TO GET BACK TO MY RATION STAMPS NOW.
JE T'AIME, JO

* THE FISH IS AN APRIL FOOL'S DAY JOKE.

* THE MILICE FRANÇAISE, OR FRENCH MILITIA, FOUGHT AGAINST THE FRENCH RESISTANCE.

FACE THE COUNTER!
HOTEL DU CHEVAL BLANC
GARAGE
BEAT IT, KID.
WHAT DO YOU WANT WITH MONSIEUR JEAN?
I HAVE A LETTER FOR HIM. BUT IT'S FOR HIS EYES ONLY.
NICE JOB, KID. IF WE NEED YOU AGAIN, WE'LL LET YOU KNOW. FOR NOW, GO HOME.

HOW MUCH FOR YOUR BOOK ON PÉTAIN? THE ONE IN THE WINDOW.
Signal
PETAIN
JEAN THOUVENIN
Le Journal de la Dr
Débarquement massif anglo-améri sur la côte normande
THE BOOK ON THE MARSHAL? ER . . . FORTY FRANCS.
ALL RIGHT THEN. I'LL BUY IT, BUT I'M NOT TAKING IT. LEAVE IT IN THE WINDOW, IF YOU DON'T MIND.
WITH THIS TAG ON IT, OF COURSE.
LA FRANCE NOUVELLE - IV
PETAIN
SOLD!
JEAN THOUVENIN
WELL . . . I'D RATHER SET IT ASIDE, IF YOU DON'T MIND.
NEVER MIND, THEN. NO SENSE DROPPING FORTY FRANCS. IN A FEW WEEKS I'LL COME IN AND TAKE WHAT I WANT.
MANCELI
SEE YOU VERY SOON, MONSIEUR MANCELIER.

JO!
omptes Mancelier
8 juillet 1944
JO, WAKE UP!
?!
OH, IT'S YOU, MAURICE. YOU'RE UP AT THIS HOUR? WHAT'S WRONG?
THEY'RE GONE!
THE GERMANS ARE GONE!
56

* PARIS LIBERATED
* PARIS WELCOMES DE GAULLE
* THE GERMAN GARRISON SURRENDERS
* LIBERATION

MARCADET
POISSONNIERS
METROPOLITAIN
URES
MACHI
A
ECRIR

1041
POST
58

BOULANGERIE
Coiffeur pour Homme
Joffo - Coiffeur

TO ALL THE JOFFO FATHERS

THE END KRIS – BAILLY – JOFFO